What's the difference?

THE MAGIC TOYSHOP

Phil Roxbee Cox & Jenny Tyler

Designed by Amanda Barlow

Photographed by Howard Allman
and Ray Moller

Edited by Rupert Heath

Photographic Magic: John Russell
Assistant designer: Rachel Kirkland

Dear Reader

Shhh! Can you keep a secret?

People have noticed strange things going on
at THE MAGIC TOYSHOP. They think that the toys
change and move about all by themselves...
But really we're doing it! (Don't tell anyone will you?)

As you go through this book you will see pairs
of pictures that look the same. But when you look
more closely you'll find LOTS of differences.

See if you can spot them all.

There are also open jack-in-the-boxes, at least
one on every page. Can you find them?

signed
   THE GREENIES

P.S. Look out for us too. We're really good at hiding.

4

Find a red steam engine and 5 ducks.

How many yellow cars are there?

5

Can you spot 10 or more differences among the dolls and teddies?

6

Find 4 teddies without scarves or bows.

Find 11 red cars.

How many buses are there?

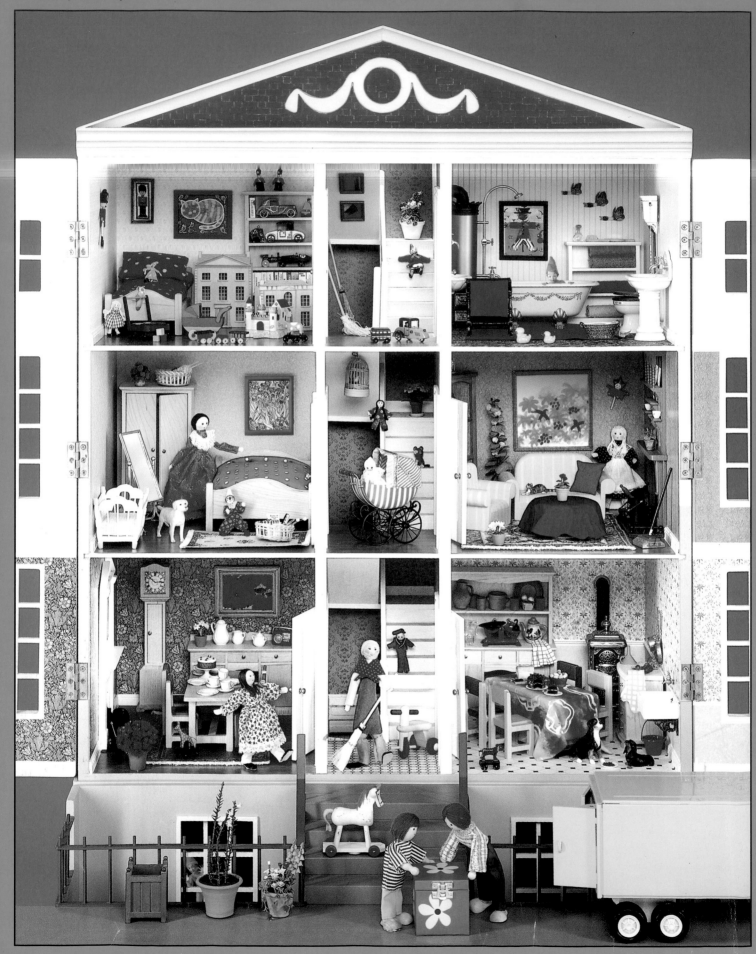

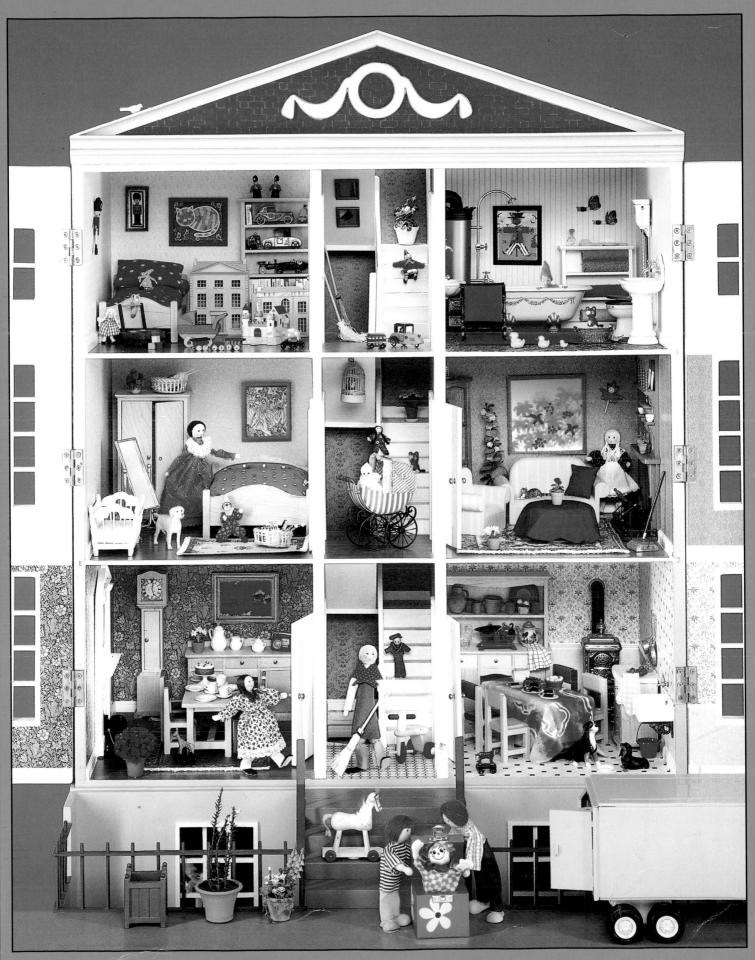

Find 3 dogs and a toy boat.

Find a black piglet.

Find Little Red Riding Hood and 3 birds.

Can you spot 10 or more differences among the creepy crawlies?

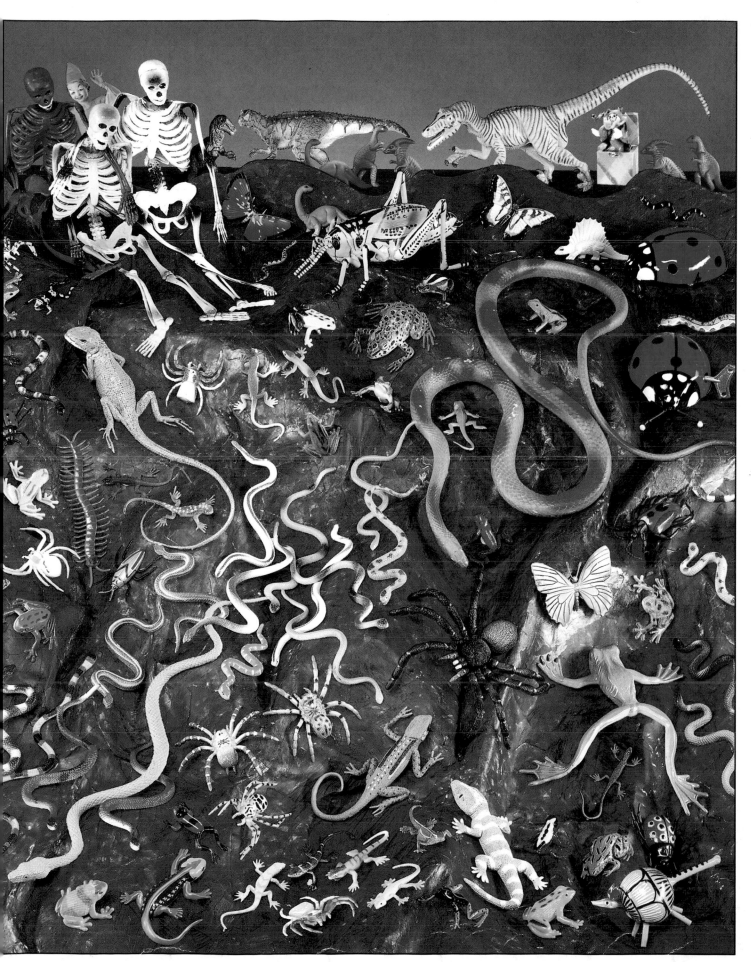

Find 3 butterflies and 6 spiders.

Can you spot 10 or more differences at the puppet show?

Find an eye patch and a violin.

Find 3 frogs and 4 golf balls.

21

Can you spot 10 or more differences in the dolls' shop?

Find a square cake, a cauliflower and a jar of strawberry jam.   23

Find 2 kazoos, 3 xylophones and 4 castanets.

Find a shark and an anchor.

How many starfish are there?

ANSWERS

Did you spot all the
differences?
Each one is circled.
Those naughty
Greenies have
diamond shapes
around them, so now
they are easy to find.

Train Table   pages 4 and 5

Dolls and Teddies   pages 6 and 7

Car Corner   pages 8 and 9

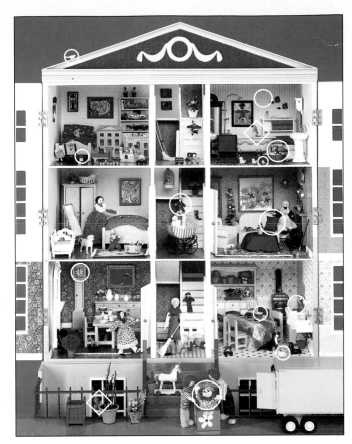

Dolls' House pages 10 and 11

Farm Table pages 12 and 13

Carnival Corner pages 14 and 15

Creepy Crawlies pages 16 and 17

Puppet Show pages 18 and 19

Sports Section pages 20 and 21

Dolls' Shop   pages 22 and 23

Music Corner   pages 24 and 25

Sea Shelves   pages 26 and 27

ACKNOWLEDGEMENTS

We wish to thank the following for permission to use their products in The Magic Toyshop.

(All addresses in the U.K. unless otherwise stated.)

Jack-in-the-Box Company, Unit 2B, Leroy House, 436 Essex Road, London, N1 3QP
Jack-in-the-Boxes

Honeysuckle Toys, Woodlands Ledge Hill, Market Lavington, SN10 4NW
Dolls' house and accessories

Dijon Ltd, The Old Print Works, Streatfield Road, Heathfield, TN21 8HX
Dolls' house accessories

Quality Dolls' House Miniatures, 55 Celandine Avenue, Priory Park, Locksheath, SO31 6WZ
Dolls' house accessories

Bodo Hennig Puppenmöbel GmbH, S7499 Wildpoldsried, Germany
Dolls' house accessories

Tony Hooper, 3 Bunting Close, Ogwell, Newton Abbot, TQ12 6BU
Dolls' house accessories

Sue Austen Miniatures, Folly End Farm, Ashton Lane, Bishops Waltham, SO32 1FQ
Dolls' house accessories

Skipper Yachts Ltd, The Granary, Dock Lane, Melton, IP12 1PE
Model boats

Worlds Apart Ltd, 4 Union Court, 18-20 Union Road, London, SW4 6JP
Kites

Early Learning Centre Ltd, Southmarston Park, Swindon, SN3 4TJ
Musical instruments and sports equipment

Bontempi Comus (U.K.) Ltd, 12 Churchill Way, Lomeshaye Industrial Estate, Nelson, BB9 6RT
Musical instruments

Brio Ltd, Messenger Close, Loughborough, LE11 5SP
Wooden trains, accessories and animals

Kidsplay, 154 Graham Road, London, SW19 3SG
Plastic and wooden animals

Merrythought Ltd, Ironbridge, Telford, TF8 7NJ
Teddy bears

Sevi, Pontives 37, I-39046 Ortisei, Südtirol, Italy
Wooden toys

Tobar Ltd, St. Margaret, Harleston, IP20 0PJ
Wooden and tin toys, novelties

Exico Ltd, 43-51 New North Road, London, N1 6JD
Wooden toys

Britain's Petite Ltd, Chelsea Street, New Baysford, Nottingham, NG7 7HR
Farmyard animals and accessories

Sigikid, H.Scharrer & Koch GmbH & Co. KG. AM Wolfsgarten 8, D-95511 Mistelbach, Germany
Soft toys

Trullala, Dornestr.17, D-23558 Lübeck, Germany
Puppets

Dreamkid Ltd, 26 Old Kenton Road, London, NW9 9NA
Dolls

Max Zapf Creations U.K., Dropshort Cottage, Orton, Kettering, NN14 1LL
Dolls

Peartree Lane Dolls, 14 Hawthorn Way, Storrington, Pulborough, RH20 4NL
Rag dolls

Alicia Merrett, 43 Anson Road, London, N7 0AR
Rag dolls

Joanna Pope, Old Church House, Church Road, Wilstead, MK45 3HH
Fairy dolls

Bburago, Riko International Ltd, 13-15A High Street, Hemel Hempstead, HP1 3AD
Cars

Corgi Ltd, Harcourt Way, Meridian Park, Leicester, LE3 2RL
Vehicles

Natural World, 33-41 The Promenade, Cheltenham, GL50 1LE
Model animals

Thanks also to the following Greenies:

Nadia Allman, Nicole Cason-Marcus, Edward Goldsmith, Emily-Rose Goldsmith, Emily Kirby-Jones, Jamie Manton

and to face painter Caro Childs.

Please note: The inclusion of a product in The Magic Toyshop does not necessarily imply that it is a toy, or that it is suitable for use by children. A variety of products shown are models or collectables and are not intended to meet child safety standards.
Every effort has been made to trace the manufacturers of the products featured in this book. If any acknowledgements have been omitted, the publishers offer their apologies and will rectify this in any subsequent editions of The Magic Toyshop, following notification.